EMOTIONOMICS 2.0

The Emotional Dynamics Underlying Key Business Goals

A guidebook with access to the Emotionomics 2.0 audio files

Dan Hill, Ph.D.,
in conversation with Tim Houlihan & Kurt Nelson,
hosts of the podcast *Behavioral Grooves*

SENSORY
LOGIC

SENSORY LOGIC®

Sensory Logic Books
www.SensoryLogic.com
1969 Stanford Avenue
St. Paul, MN 55105 USA

For information about special discounts for bulk purchases, contact Sensory Logic, Inc.
at 651.434.9285 or dhill@sensorylogic.com.

ISBN 13: 978-0-9997416-6-5

Printed in the United States of America

Book cover and interior design by JamesMonroeDesign.com

Contents

To access the *Emotionomics 2.0* audio files:

1) Open your camera/QR code reader. 2) Hold your device over this QR Code.
3) Follow instructions to complete the action.

Introduction:
Why Now, What Has & Hasn't Changed

Why (a New Edition) Now?

Just as the original edition of *Emotionomics* was hitting the bookstores, the Great Recession began, leading to the largest economic downturn since World War Two. Now with the impact of Covid-19 still playing out, the business world is navigating what's been called the Great Resignation or the Great Reshuffle as employees change jobs and sometimes entire careers. Covid-19 is the biggest pandemic humanity has faced since the end of World War One. It's not just a health crisis, however; it's also a call to arms to re-invent capitalism *to make it warmer, more inclusive and fairer* to resolve the crisis in capitalism ignited by the Great Recession.

What (Else) Has Changed (from 2007 to 2022)?

The rise of social media (and Gen Z activism), digitization, automation, Big Data, and of late the possible re-trenching of globalization as "near-shoring" and "re-shoring" becomes common business terms alongside "off-shoring" and "out-sourcing." Add to that list an emphasis not only on CX (the customer experience) but now also on EX (the employee experience), both of which are inherently and profoundly emotional in nature.

What Hasn't Changed?

What we feel always drives behavior. The impetus for *Emotionomics* was the new scientific estimate that over 95% of people's mental activity is sensory-emotive and intuitive (laying waste to the fallacy that we're rational decision-makers). As a mental model, Mr. Spock of *Star Trek* fame needs to step aside to make room for Homer Simpson. There are two currencies: dollar and emotions, and to capture the former you have to leverage the latter wisely.

Part 1

Orientation & Context

CHAPTER 1
Adaptability: Emotions, EQ & Facial Coding

Goal #1: Engage Prospective Buyers & Hires

For companies to succeed, they need to optimize (emotional) engagement. In simplest terms, motivating people is the key. How basic can you get? The problem is that left their own devices, people resemble house cats. They prefer lying in the sun. You need to spark their curiosity and get them to open their eyes to consider what you're offering. The problem is that companies (like people) are often selfish and not very good at focusing on what's in it for others. Failing to motivate people is like trying to sell a fancy car on the dealer lot while forgetting to put any (emotional) fuel in the tank for the test drive.

Goal #2: Promote Loyalty

Compared to getting people to stay on-board, attracting their attention and interest seems easy. To break through the clutter, after all, your best means is usually to leverage the emotions of surprise (curiosity) plus happiness or at least the hope of happiness that comes from buying the product or accepting the job. Can you create a wow sufficient to reel them in? Afterwards, however, negative emotions like anger (resentment), fear (discomfort), contempt (distrust) and sadness (disappointment) can all rear their ugly heads. Companies that are *emotionally literate* will enjoy about a 6% advantage in navigating trouble, but does your company qualify?

Goal #3: Leverage Face Time

Leonardo da Vinci was the first great facial coder. Check out his notebooks with drawings of facial muscles and the emotions they reveal. Everyone knows that in-person, face-time talks move business forward, but do leaders, managers, and salespeople know what kind of signals are present? To look *but not see* leads to squandered opportunities.

Pop Quiz—What Do Emotions Mean?

Instructions: Match each emotion to whichever meaning fits it best.

Emotion	Meaning (Options)
1. Sadness	A. Fulfillment
2. Fear	B. Attention
3. Happiness	C. Risk
4. Disgust	D. Control
5. Anger	E. Rejection
6. Contempt	F. Disappointment
7. Surprise	G. Distrust

(Correct answers: 1F, 2C, 3A, 4E, 5D, 6G, 7B)

CHAPTER 2
Branding: Externally & Internally Aligned

Goal #1: Establish a Purpose-Driven Brand

The original edition of *Emotionomics* addressed a world in which Baby Boomers and Gen X predominated. By contrast, *Emotionomics 2.0* addresses a world in which Millennials and Gen Z now constitute the ever-growing majority of consumers and employees alike. Companies used to focus on their "unique value proposition." Today, a company's values—capitalism with a heart and moral compass—stand front and center. The challenge is that cynics may come to (rightly) distrust a company's professed values as merely a matter of lip-service.

Goal #2: Link Favorable Hot-Button Associations

Companies with a notable founder (e.g., Walt Disney, Steve Jobs) have an inherent edge. Their founder's personality is memorable enough to serve as a jumping-off point. Other companies, however, struggle to create a myth that lifts a brand from factual origin (often a superior offer) to fictional status, whereby storytelling adds an emotional halo around a branded offer that's no longer functionally better. A great tagline, logo or projected sense of place (e.g., Ralph Lauren's aura of serving people who enjoy a *Great-Gatsby* lifestyle) can do the trick.

Goal #3: Resolve Scandals with the Right PR

When a scandal erupts, who should serve as the company's public face in front of the media? The answer is that gender biases and status impact the choices. Based on the track record of how companies' stocks perform afterwards, the solution is a guy if it's an operational error; a woman if it's an error involving the company's culture; and the CEO if it's a disaster on an epic scale where anybody of lesser rank just won't do. In every case, showing sadness—real contrition—makes the apology viable.

Pop Quiz—Which Brand Best Personifies Each Archetype?

Instructions: Match each brand to whichever archetype fits it best.

Brand	Archetype (Options)
1. Amazon	A. Creator
2. Apple	B. Caregiver
3. Google	C. Ruler
4. Facebook	D. Jester
5. McDonalds	E. Regular Guy/Gal
6. Louis Vuitton	F. Lover
7. Disney	G. Hero
8. Tiktok	H. Outlaw
9. Tesla	I. Magician
10. LinkedIn	J. Innocent
11. Pampers	K Explorer
12. Nike	L. Sage

(Correct answers: 1C, 2A, 3L, 4F, 5E, 6I, 7J, 8D, 9H, 10K, 11B, 12G)

Part 2

Marketplace Applications

CHAPTER 3

Innovation: Democratizing the Creative Process

Goal #1: Ensure Innovation Happens (at All)

Talk about a major statistical disconnect. Surveyed executives signal that their companies' future success depends on innovation (84%) and yet only 6% of them are satisfied with the pace of innovation at the firms they lead. Ouch. What are the three biggest factors undermining innovation? The first is *a lack of coordination* (i.e, bureaucratic silos) as departments fight to defend their own turf. The other two factors also have an emotional component: *a lack of creativity* (little delight in brainstorming) goes along with *a paralyzing fear of failure*.

Goal #2: Commit to Inspiring Creativity

One solution is to hire people who exhibit—in spades—the personality trait of being open to experience. Curiosity and pride in original, divergent thinking are crucial attributes to nurture. Meanwhile, on a group basis so is getting employees' competitive juices flowing. To promote progress, enable internal teams to take inspiration from customer feedback and supplier input alike in staging idea days, hackathons and other events where trophies get awarded and reputations get made as new concepts emerge.

Goal #3: Sponsor & Support Cooperation

Let's admit that the fear of failure limiting the pace of innovation isn't merely a matter of one's own fear. There's collective fear, too. The social dimension of fear moves beyond individual regret to also being afraid of getting embarrassed in front of others. Who likes to "look dumb"? Therefore, a support structure needs to be in place, involving creativity gurus, innovation coordinators, and really most important of all—an innovation council of mentors prepared to champion fresh ideas and overcome the inertia of settling for the status quo.

Pop Quiz—Per Sector, Which Emotion Tests Above Norm?

Instructions: Match each sector to whichever option(s) fits best, based on which emotions are more prevalent on average per sector. Note that for some sectors, more than one emotion will apply.

Sector

1. Technology (products)
2. Retail (settings)
3. Office (products)
4. Automotive
5. Alcohol

Emotion (Options)

A. Fear
B. Disgust
C. Anger
D. Sadness
E. Skepticism (doubting smile)
F. Surprise
G. Joy (true smile)

(Correct answers: 1E/G, 2F, 3B, 4C/D, 5A)

CHAPTER 4

Marketing: Ads Are Now a Smaller Part of the Mix

Goal #1: Launch Advertising That Achieves ROI

When 19th century department store owner John Wannamaker famously said, "Half my advertising dollar is wasted, but I don't know which half," the guy was actually too optimistic. Studies done 20 years ago found that about 2/3rds of all advertising performed well-to-okay, while 1/3rd caused *a decline* in sales. Starting in 2009, however, the amount of "digital noise" created by individuals through social media surpassed the "promotional noise" created by companies—and has grown exponentially ever since. As a result, the amount of advertising that can deliver ROI may now be as low as 5%. Testing ads through conventional online surveys or focus groups makes that predicament even worse. Why? *Consumers don't think their feelings; they feel them.* So traditional research methods run the huge risk of being off-base by capturing only if the ads are on-message, and not if they're also on-emotion.

Goal #2: Make Good Use of Limited Time

In a TV spot or online video, attention typically craters during the last 3–5 seconds (when the company's logo appears). What's the remedy? With video, emotional engagement peaks on average twice: once about 10 seconds in, and again just before the branded closing. So why not insert brand signifiers earlier than later, to improve your odds of success.

Goal #3: Market Only in Ways That Matter

The old model was build/market/sell, leading to lots of embedded costs up front. In contrast, Tesla offers a new way forward: market/sell/build, and then market some more to affirm your customers bought wisely. Yes, promote a brand that offers a overriding purpose (in Tesla's case, to reduce global warming), get the sale, and only then custom-build what your customers want.

Pop Quiz—How Best to Reach Your Target Market?

Instructions: There are four possible outcomes, of which two are desirable. Which combinations avoid stress or being too dull?

Possible Outcomes

1. Too Stressful

2. Too Dull

3. Winning Formula #1

4. Winning Formula #2

Formula (Options)

A. Complexity

B. Familiarity

C. Novelty

D. Simplicity

(Correct answers: 1A/C, 2B/D, 3A/B, 4C/D)

CHAPTER 5

Sales: Detecting the Ability & Willingness to Pay

Goal #1: Avoid Huge Turn-Over in Your Salesforce

On average, the annual turn-over rate among companies' salesforces lands somewhere in the range of 25% (double the general workforce rate). Here's a trick question: is a good salesperson more likely to be an extrovert or an introvert? The answer lies halfway in between because a good salesperson (upbeat, resilient, and caring) is likely to be an ambivert instead. Nowadays, being brash isn't enough; you've got to prove you understand your prospects' needs and that you're not just a hunter eager to turn them into prey. Otherwise, you won't last long.

Goal #2: Become a Trusted Curator of Knowledge

Welcome to the cat-and-mouse era of sales. In short, while salespeople turn into internet sleuths to identify prospects and their needs, prospects are in turn looking to confirm the relevancy and value of the salesperson's offer before bothering to take a phone call or meeting. Trust is indeed the emotion of business—and establishing yourself as an expert will require proof points given by offering curated insights *upfront* to get the ball rolling.

Goal #3: Close More Deals by Customizing

The typical pitch deck gets it all-wrong. It's me-me-me (all about your company's offer). Shorten the deck and leave time to figure out which motivation you can best leverage to close the deal. Will it be *greed* (the prospect is seeking a company or personal reward)? *Envy* (the prospect is status conscious)? *Pride* (the prospect wants to be seen as a winner)? Or is it *fear* (the hesitant prospect is even more afraid of the cost of inaction)? Figure out the answer or lose out.

Pop Quiz—What Non-Verbal Clues Are Evident?

Instructions: Match the middle and right column entries to the emotion being exhibited.

Emotions	Voice—Pitch & Range	Facial Expressions
1. Anger	A. High & Wide	AA. Lifts
2. Disgust	B. Low & Narrow	BB. Compression
3. Fear	C. Low & Wide	CC. Droops
4. Happiness		DD. Recoils
5. Sadness		EE. Blanches

(Correct answers: 1A/BB, 2C/DD, 3A/EE, 4A/AA, 5B/CC)

CHAPTER 6

CX: Help Customers Experience a Satisfying Wow

Goal #1: Make the Shopping Experience Engaging

As shoppers, which of our 5 senses get utilized most often? Sight and sound are the default modes, and all that websites can rely on. Make your site highly visual and set up like a fast-food restaurant to facilitate instant gratification. If on the other hand we're talking about the retail experience, invoke smell, taste and especially *touch* when feasible. Research shows that those 3 senses can create an emotional engagement level 3x higher than sight alone. Get a shopper to linger and *hold* onto the product, and you're golden.

Goal #2: Turn Customer Problems into Opportunities

Let's get real. Customers come to the Customer Service department because they *haven't* gotten the service they expected. The offer or support for the offer was lacking and didn't meet expectations. Solving the immediate problem shouldn't be the goal, however. You need to fix the customers even more so. They feel like a fool for having bought unwisely. Showing respect and reaffirming their worth comes ahead of being knowledgeable or helpful, and the means to making an unhappy customer a loyal one instead.

Goal #3: Turn Customer Service into a Profit Center

Customer Service has long been seen as a cost-center, a place to get by on as low a budget as possible. Well, being cheap doesn't create good feelings. What's a better approach? Turn CS into a source of innovation. There are Annual Employee and Annual Stockholder meetings. Why not also host Annual Customer meetings? Gain feedback, try out new ideas. Invite suppliers, too. Most of all, re-cast the department staff as brand ambassadors. They know the problems customers experience first-hand; now let them lend a hand in arriving at superior solutions.

Pop Quiz—What Creates Frustrated Customers?

Instructions: Match the type of consumer experience to the correct, corresponding amount of frustration it causes.

Touch Point		Amount of Frustration	
1.	Packaging	A.	38%
2.	Print Ads	B.	32%
3.	Product Usage	C.	28%
4.	TV Spots	D.	26%
5.	Websites	E.	24%

(Correct answers: 1E, 2D, 3B, 4C, 5A)

Part 3

Workplace Applications

CHAPTER 7
Leadership: Taking a More Inclusive Role

Goal #1: Protect the Company from Tunnel Vision

The statistics are startling. Only 36% of business professionals believe their companies foster an inclusive culture. At the same time though, companies with more diverse executive teams enjoy 19% higher revenue thanks to greater innovation. What's going on here? What are the odds that white, male leaders are choosing their own *comfort level* over-and-above ROI (and their own, therefore rising stock options)? To increase empathy and diversity, what's a solution? Experiences, not slide decks! Hit the road. Get out of the corner office. Try executive immersion excursions to understand consumer segments executives otherwise rarely interact with.

Goal #2: Create a More Engaged Work Culture

Here's another striking statistic: only 16% of employees are fully engaged on the job. What will it take to turn that situation around? The answer starts at the top because as much as 30% of the emotional climate at companies gets created by the CEO. What distinguishes effective U.S. presidents and democratic versus autocratic leaders around the globe? The trait of openness to experience is key, plus a tendency to feel happy versus being prone to anger and disgust.

Goal #3: Improve the Success Rate of M & A Activity

The majority of mergers and acquisitions fail to achieve their financial targets. A major reason is that during the process, workers get distracted by fear and then, later, succumb to despair. Meanwhile, the leadership team risks being oblivious as it huddles with lawyers, accountants, and outside consultants. What needs to change? Get the input of informal, *internal* leaders within the ranks besides talking face-to-face with other employees as often as possible.

Pop Quiz—Which Emotions Distinguish Good from Bad CEOs?

Instructions: From the column of emotions, select the option that best fits each of the scenarios. The first two involve the company's stock price while the CEO is in office, whereas misdeeds reference the CEO engaging in sexual, legal or financial misconduct. Note that an emotion can be chosen more than once.

Scenarios

1. Emotion is common—stock performs well
2. Emotion rare—stock performs poorly
3. Emotion is common—CEO misdeeds
4. Emotion rare—CEO misdeeds

Emotions

A. Anger
B. Contempt
C. Curiosity
D. Disgust
E. Fear
F. Happiness
G. Sadness

(Correct answers: 1C, 2F, 3B, 4F)

CHAPTER 8
Managers: Become the Cultivators of Talent

Goal #1: Secure & Retain Talent

Employees get hired by managers and often leave because of them, too. At both ends of the narrative, start and finish, what are managers possibly doing wrong? Up front, they're likely to be discounting the importance of curiosity and tolerance-for-ambiguity as vital attributes in their hiring choices. On the back side, if they've failed to show enough agility and emotional intelligence (EQ) to retain talent, at least they could mitigate their losses. Why not encourage departing workers to stay in touch, akin to how colleges leverage alumni networks.

Goal #2: Help Your Staff Realize Its Potential

The bad news is that an estimated 25% of all bosses qualify as bullies. Their staffs suffer from stress and under-performance follows. The good news is there's a model with 3 conditions a company's workforce needs to perform well: a feasible amount of *autonomy*, an opportunity to achieve some degree of *mastery* on the job, and a sense of *purpose* that turns one's workday efforts into meaningful activities.

Goal #3: Benefit More from Collaboration

The pitfalls of most employees' work lives are tedious, unproductive meetings and too many emails. Put in emotional terms: while disgust is having a bad taste in your mouth, boredom is caused by having *no taste* at all. Most meetings and emails aren't exactly lip-smacking treats. Improvement opportunities abound. Hold fewer and shorter meetings. Have a clear agenda. Handle all emails during two or three blocks of time in the day, rather than letting them serve as constant distractions. Most of all, keep the team sizes small so that in collaborating on projects, there's real comradery and accountability alike.

Pop Quiz—What Do These Behaviors Trigger?

Instructions: These are 10 types of behaviors managers might engage in during conversations with their staff members. Decide which 5 behaviors spur positive, oxytocin, bonding reactions and which 5 behaviors instead spur negative, cortisol, stress reactions in staff members. Also try ranking the behaviors from high-to-low based on the amount of either oxytocin or cortisol they create.

Neurochemical Reactions

1. Oxytocin (most to least amount)

2. Cortisol (most to least amount)

Manager Behavior

A. Concern for others

B. Don't trust others' intentions

C. Emotions detract from listening

D. Focused on convincing others

E. Open to difficult conversations

F. Others are not understanding

G. Paint picture of mutual success

H. Pretend to be listening

I. Stimulate discussion/curiosity

J. Truthful about what's on mind

(Correct answers: For #1, A, J, I, G, E; for #2, B, D, F, H, C)

CHAPTER 9
EX: Navigating a 2-Way Street

Goal #1: Ensure a Good Fit for New Hires

Job prospects should help managers improve the interview process by asking questions to determine mutual compatibility. Options include: how does it feel to be at this company and in this department? What will I learn in this role? How can my potential be realized? Will I have the opportunity to create something new? What are the potential stumbling blocks? *And all importantly*, what kind of colleagues and contacts will I have? Then it's up to the manager to build momentum by installing an on-boarding process that provides plenty of guidance and feedback, including biweekly orientation conferences for the first 2—3 months on the job.

Goal #2: Minimize the Toxicity of Office Politics

Never forget that your career is a perception game: what you perceive, and how you are (fairly or unfairly) perceived by others. Together, managers and their staffs can try to preserve morale and avoid debilitating "sniping" by keeping people focused on 3 criteria that can serve as an objective roadmap everyone can agree on. First, focus on *competency*—how well each job is getting done. Second, safeguard long-term viability by examining *commitment* levels to figure out what adds or drains employees' energy levels. Third, increase *affinity* by figuring out who gets along with whom best and under which circumstances, and then plan accordingly.

Goal #3: Reduce Job Burn-Out

When employees burn out, energy levels and quality standards drop. What increases? Cynicism and fear as employees hide on the job. If the cause is a felt lack of appreciation, then events like gratitude lunches held off-site may help. If however the cause of burn-out is a lack of support in a role with crushing demands, then try rotating or rebalancing assignments instead.

Pop Quiz—Who's a Drag at Work?

Instructions: Below are 10 types of colleagues. From the emotion options, decide which one is most likely to characterize these colleagues. Note that each emotion may apply more than once.

Type of Colleague	Characteristic Emotion
1. Amy Attitude (brings everyone down)	A. Anger
2. Antagonist (rude/unpleasant)	B. Contempt
3. Blameless Bob (always has an excuse)	C. Fear
4. Early Retiree (on-the-job slacking)	D. Happiness
5. Hand-Holder (needs constant help)	E. Sadness
6. Insubordinate Subordinate (creates scenes)	
7. Thumb-Twiddler (lacks initiative)	
8. Tortoise (shows up late or not at all)	
9. Whiner (always complains)	
10. Worrywart (personal problems infringe)	

(Correct answers: 1E, 2A, 3D, 4D, 5C, 6B, 7E, 8E, 9E, 10C)

Epilogue: Selected Highlights

What Did Tim & Kurt Choose?

- Branding—In essence declare *who* are as a company, what's your personality and values, with your identity affirmed by a constellation of hot-button associations.

- Innovation—The great inhibitor is fear, which must be overcome both individually and collectively with the help of mentors and a supportive operational structure.

- Marketing—The Tesla model of securing the customer before you produce the offer isn't the new version of just-in-time manufacturing, it's also a sign that marketing must likewise be customized to address individual needs.

- Sales—With so much noise out there, it's never been more important to separate the wheat-from-the-chaff for prospects and to do so in a manner that builds trust.

- CX—Companies should hold annual, even quarterly, customer conferences attended by executives, the sales team, and anyone intent on innovation and optimization.

- Leadership—Gen Z represents the first instance where the majority of employees are non-white; will executives be capable of not leaving them feeling marginalized?

- Managers—The value of tracking the company's Return on Mistakes (ROM) should be a championed metric to overcome the tendency to hide costly mistakes instead.

- EX: Real engagement can only come from getting a fair opportunity to control one's destiny, making contributions that honor your sense of selfhood.

The Participants' Profiles

Dan Hill, Ph.D, is as the president of Sensory Logic, Inc., which has conducted market research for over half of the world's top 100 B2C companies. Hill pioneered the use of facial coding to capture and quantify consumers' and employees' emotional responses and is a certified Facial Action Coding System (FACS) practitioner with 7 U.S. patents. He's also the author of 9 previous books, including *Emotionomics*, which was chosen by *Advertising Age* as one of the top-ten must-read books of 2009 and features a foreword by Sam Simon, co-creator of *The Simpsons*. Hill's TV appearances have included: ABC's "Good Morning, America," NBC's "The Today Show," Al Jazeera, Bloomberg TV, CNBC, CNN, ESPN, Fox, MSNBC, and PBS. Media coverage has ranged from *Advertising Age* to *Entrepreneur*, *Fast Company*, *The Financial Times*, *Forbes China*, *Inc.*, *Kiplinger's*, *The Los Angeles Times*, *The New York Times*, *Politico*, *Time*, *USA Today*, and *The Wall Street Journal*, plus having been a columnist for Reuters during the 2016 U.S. presidential race. Nowadays, Hill hosts the podcast "Dan Hill's EQ Spotlight" on the New Books Network (NBN), the world's largest book review platform.

Tim Houlihan and **Kurt Nelson**, Ph.D., co-host the podcast *Behavioral Grooves*, which reaches audiences in over 170 countries and has been acclaimed by *Habits Weekly* and *Psychology Today*. In addition, Houlihan runs BehaviorAlchemy and Nelson runs The Lantern Group. Both consulting firms are based on applying behavioral science principles to business. Previously, Houlihan worked in corporate marketing, sales, and HR settings. Following his Ph.D. from Capella University, Nelson has focused on ways to drive organizational change by positively influencing how people behave.

Other Available Resources

Based on solutions curated from both his podcast and unique market-research findings, Hill offers keynote speeches as well as workshop training and consulting services. The focus is on actionable tips and procedures for helping companies realize their potential. For specifics (including sample testimonials), go to www.sensorylogic.com and click on Speaking.

These three recent books provide additional learnings:

Famous Faces Decoded: A Guidebook for Reading Others - Unless you've never been lied to in life, you know that words aren't enough in assessing people and situations. Vital to emotional intelligence is fluently reading facial expressions. Using celebrity examples from Hollywood, music, sports, politics and business, this book provides insights relevant to applications ranging from hiring to sales, negotiations, and interacting with your boss, colleagues and customers.

Two Cheers for Democracy: How Emotions Drive Leadership Style - How might the personalities of CEOs impact their effectiveness on the job? Clues are available by studying U.S. presidents and notable foreign leaders. Here, emotional patterns and characteristic traits are correlated to the benchmarks of presidential greatness rankings, Gallup poll results taken after presidential debates, and whether leaders proved to be democratic or authoritarian. What emerges are the qualities required to exhibit both flexibility and resilience in building rapport with others.

Blah Blah Blah: A Snarky Guide to Office Lingo - The role of satire is to mock and, thereby, correct perceived wrongs. Since business cliches often inadvertently reveal flawed beliefs and behaviors detrimental to a company's culture and performance, these diabolical definitions implicitly suggest what constructive change can look like.